XF   Couvillon, Alice.
COU   Evangeline for children

Evangeline
for Children

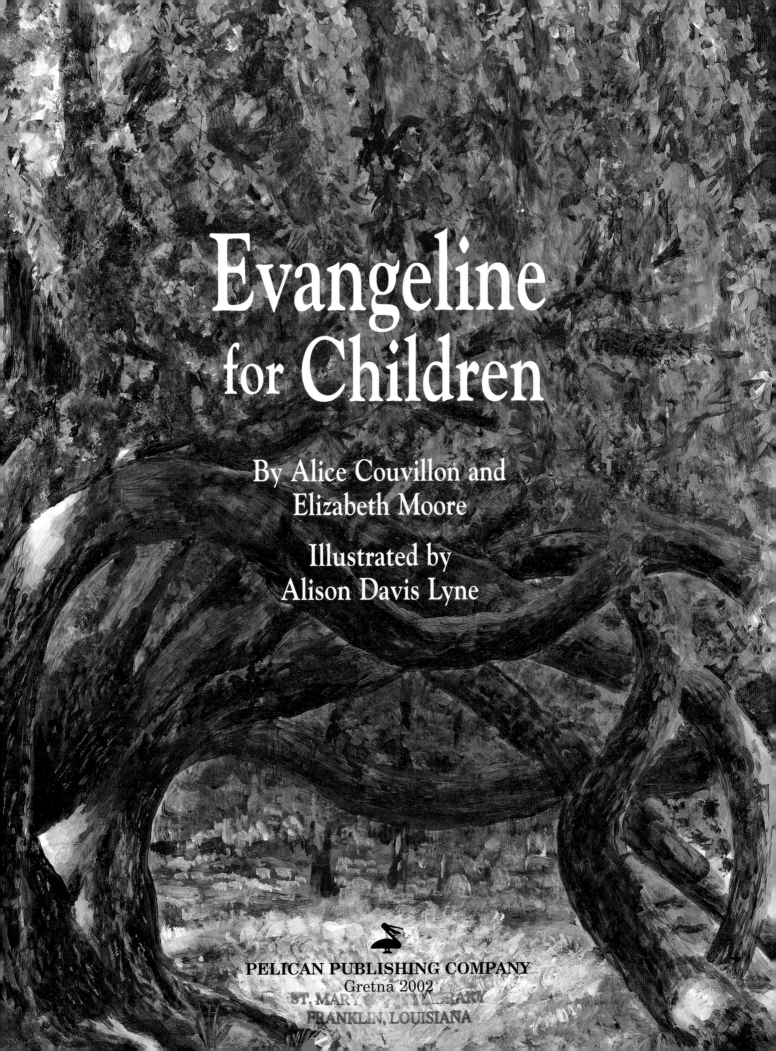

Evangeline
for Children

By Alice Couvillon and
Elizabeth Moore

Illustrated by
Alison Davis Lyne

PELICAN PUBLISHING COMPANY
Gretna 2002

ST. MARY PARISH LIBRARY
FRANKLIN, LOUISIANA

The word "Pelican" and the depiction of a pelican are
trademarks of Pelican Publishing Company, Inc., and are
registered in the U.S. Patent and Trademark Office.

Library of Congress Cataloging-in-Publication Data

Couvillon, Alice.
  Evangeline for children / written by Alice Couvillon and Elizabeth
Moore ; illustrated by Alison Davis Lyne.
    p. cm.
  Summary: Retells in prose Henry Wadsworth Longfellow's epic poem
about a young woman's search for her lover, Gabriel, after the Acadian
exile from Canada.
  ISBN 1-56554-709-8 (alk. paper)
    [1. Acadians—Fiction.] I. Moore, Elizabeth. II. Lyne, Alison D., ill.
III. Longfellow, Henry Wadsworth, 1807-1882. Evangeline. IV. Title.

PZ7.C8334 Ev 2000
[E]—dc21

                                                                99-057101

Printed in Hong Kong

Published by Pelican Publishing Company, Inc.
1000 Burmaster Street, Gretna, Louisiana 70053

Evangeline for Children
EVANGELINE, A TALE OF ACADIE

Surrounded by the pines and hemlocks in the French village of Grand Pré, a peaceful people, the Acadians, once lived. The men were humble farmers, and the women tended to their families and homes.

The children played in the meadows of wild flowers and laughed in the sun. All that remains today of Grand Pré are the memories of these people as told in this tale of love and devotion.

PART THE FIRST

On the edge of the village facing the sea was a thatched-roof hut where an old farmer named Benedict lived with his beautiful daughter, Evangeline.

She was seventeen years
old, with sparkling black
eyes and soft, brown hair around
her lovely face. Many young men sought to marry Evangeline,
but her heart belonged to Gabriel, son of Basil the Blacksmith.

Basil and Benedict were best of friends, and their children grew up as brother and sister—sliding down hillsides into the meadows after winter snows and searching for nests of swallows under the warm, summer sun.

As years passed, the friendship of Evangeline and Gabriel deepened into love, and they excitedly planned their wedding. Even though enemy British ships arrived in the harbor of Grand Pré, nothing could stop the joy of their coming marriage.

The villagers gathered at Benedict's house for a party to celebrate the engagement of Evangeline and Gabriel. In a shady orchard, a fiddler tapped his wooden shoes to the music, as guests whirled around and around in dizzying dances.

The men cried out in anger, but were locked as prisoners in the church as the women sorrowfully trudged home to pack their belongings.

On the fifth day after the announcement, the women and children met at the shore in the gloomy morning light. Late in the afternoon, the weary men joined their grieving families and prepared to board the ships.

Suddenly, shouting soldiers marched through the crowds, tearing children from their mothers' arms and separating husbands from wives. Confused and scared, the Acadians screamed for their loved ones.

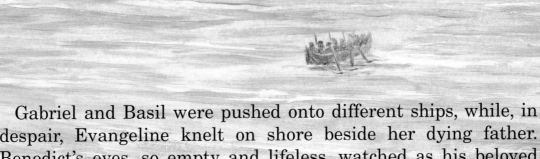

Gabriel and Basil were pushed onto different ships, while, in despair, Evangeline knelt on shore beside her dying father. Benedict's eyes, so empty and lifeless, watched as his beloved Grand Pré, torched by the British soldiers, disappeared under a blanket of smoke.

His heart broken, Benedict closed his eyes for the last time. He was buried by the sea and the last thing the Acadians saw as they sailed from their homeland was Benedict's lonely grave lit by the bright red glow of their burning village.

PART THE SECOND

The Acadians were scattered to distant lands. Hopeless and alone, they wandered from place to place, seeking word from friends and family. Among them was Evangeline, who searched endlessly for Gabriel.

She had heard rumors of his travels and learned
that he had last been seen in the lowlands of
Louisiana. Guided by hope, she sailed down the Mississippi to this
strange and dreamlike land of sluggish black bayous, waving
Spanish moss, and the heavy perfume of sweet magnolia blossoms.

On the banks of the Teche River in the town of St. Martinville, Evangeline found Basil the Blacksmith. Laughing and weeping, she hugged him and soon learned that Gabriel had left that morning on a hunting and trapping trip.

Evangeline's heart leapt with joy as she made plans to follow his path the next day. While waiting for the sunrise, she walked beneath the mighty oaks to a vast prairie twinkling with fireflies that seemed to spark glimmers of hope that soon she would be in her lover's arms.

With Indian guides to lead the way, Basil
and Evangeline traced Gabriel's course. Often,
they spied swirls of smoke from his campfire rising
through the forest, only to find burned charcoal and dying
embers the next day. They seemed so close! Weeks went by, and
Evangeline's heart became worn and weary, but she continued
her search.

At a church mission, a kind priest told Evangeline of his visit with Gabriel only six days earlier. She learned that he would return to that same mission in the fall, so, bidding farewell to Basil, she alone awaited her love.

Autumn came, then winter, but Gabriel did not come. Summer followed spring with no word. Discouraged, Evangeline once again set forth on her journey. Year after year, she searched for Gabriel. And while her youth and beauty gradually faded, her love for Gabriel never died.

As an old woman with hair the color of cold ashes, Evangeline finally abandoned her search. Her love for Gabriel blossomed into devotion for God. She took religious vows instead of wedding vows, and her life was dedicated to nursing the sick and soothing the pain of the dying.

One day, after picking wildflowers to brighten the spirits of the sick, she entered the room of an old, thin man. The flowers dropped to the floor.

For, in the shaft of sunlight, for a brief moment, his wrinkled face seemed young.

She recognized Gabriel, and cradled his head to her heart. They gazed into each other's eyes, and he breathed his last breath trying to whisper her name.

Gabriel and Evangeline, now lie side by side in nameless graves. Their long journey is complete—never united in life, their souls are now one.

EVANGELINE, AS TOLD IN PROSE AND POETRY

HISTORY OF THE ACADIANS

The Acadians, sailing from France in 1604, were among the first Europeans to reach North America, settling in Nova Scotia, Canada, sixteen years before the Mayflower arrived at Plymouth Rock. The Catholic Acadians remained loyal to France, and when Nova Scotia was given to Protestant Great Britain, following Queen Anne's War in 1713, they refused to take an oath of allegiance to the British king. Because of this, British soldiers burned down their homes and barns, and over the years, 10,000 Acadians were forcefully exiled to distant lands. Separated from family members, Acadians were crowded into ships with inadequate supplies of food and water.

Many died from smallpox and in shipwrecks. There had been no plans to relocate the people, and when the Acadians arrived in port cities on the East Coast, most were unwanted and forced back to ships bound for Europe. Those that stayed were treated cruelly, and even made to work as slaves. In all, they endured thirty years of hostile conditions and desperate searches for loved ones before the Acadians finally settled on friendly land. Spanish rulers welcomed 2,500 exiles to the swamps and bayous of Louisiana. They lived off of the land and became fishermen, hunters, and trappers.

In 1847, the poet Henry Wadsworth Longfellow wrote the epic poem "Evangeline," a story of the heroine's search for her lover, Gabriel, after the Acadian exile or *Grand Dérangement*. There are several versions of Evangeline, and it is still a mystery whether she really existed. Today, descendants of the Acadians are called "Cajuns," and they are the largest French-speaking group in the United States. They are proud of their French heritage, and like the Acadians of long ago, love to dance, sing, and tell a good story.